The Stripper Diaries

By

Trisha Paytas

Copyright © 2013 Trisha Paytas
All rights reserved.

ISBN: 1490428801
ISBN 13: 9781490428802

This ain't *The Princess Diaries*…It's *The Stripper Diaries*—funny, sad, shocking, true.

Disclaimer! I do not endorse becoming a stripper! Not that it ever sounded glamorous to me…but movies/TV/lies **whateverrrrr** make it sound like it's the best and easiest job ever. It's *not!* especially in today's strip clubs. Trust me.

Warning: this is not glamorous, and it may not make perfect sense, as it is scattered. I literally transcribed straight from the actual journals I kept at the time and really didn't hold anything back. I changed names, locations, and certain events, but everything is very real. It's dark, and it's graphic, but I wanted to present the world of stripping as it was when I was doing it, as it is today.

Having said that, I did find humor in some of my entries. Maybe it's because I lived it, and looking back on what I thought was the lowest point of my life, in the grand scheme of things, I realize it's really just a minor bump in my road. It's just something I figured I'd share.

Again, this is just a small snippet of my life as a stripper; all these entries were written in the heat of a moment. To learn more about me and my life as a whole, my first book *The History of My Insanity* goes more into who I am as a person and not just who I was as a stripper.

No judgment on strippers, as I was one. Just observations and facts.

I don't really know where I was going with this, but a lot of people do ask me about it. I'm pretty open. Stripping is bad. I am forgiven, and I'm just lucky to have gotten out. It can suck you in.

October 16, 2006

Dear Diary,

    I didn't realize it'd be this hard...Five months in Hollywood, and I'm broke and unemployed. My only friend, Brian, an assistant to a major iconic rock star, suggested a job for me, a job he told me could make a lot of money and fast. I did tonight what I never thought I'd do...I became a stripper. I hate it! I hate being naked—I hate people touching me for twenty dollars anywhere they want, but I'm a star! I literally wouldn't even get my clothes back on before another guy wanted a dance. Sure, they smell bad, but for the most part, I explained I was new and pretty much just danced in front of them with an occasional boob grab—ouchie though. They want me to work tomorrow, and after making three hundred dollars tonight, I'm tempted...

    I think Presley was a good choice of name. I get a lot of older guys with that one. It also lets me dance to Elvis whenever I want—which is awesome. My heels from my graduation are going to get way too worn out though; got to find me some of the big chunky ones... Guess I'll Google that. Also need to find pole lessons. I had no idea what to do on stage. Only need this for a couple more months to get back on my feet. Still continuing my prayer book and going to auditions and school. Got it under control. Should also invest in some hair extensions and string bikinis. My old navy swimsuit is just not as sexy as the other girls'.

    High hopes and superduper optimistic! Seems like pretty easy money...I guess what they say about strippers is true. They make bank—I'm going to make an appointment for headshots next week! Finally. Wouldn't it be awesome if Quentin Tarantino or Burt Reynolds came in one day? I heard they get celebrities in there a lot. How cool, huh? Hopefully, the touching will calm down after a few nights.

Love,

T

October 20, 2006

Dear Diary,

 I got extensions today! Oh yeah! I felt so sexy on stage. It's so fun to actually be doing what all the sexy girls do. This is amazing. Made about a hundred dollars, and it was just fun. Just dancing to Elvis and feeling like a Barbie. So many compliments from guys, it feels so good. It really does. I tell everyone I'm a virgin, and they don't care. They still want me to dance for them. It's nice to be able to have my morals and just dance. No drugs, no sex, just fun times at a strip club. Sometimes, I like to pretend I'm in a Motley Crue video, just doing some serious hairography.

 So this guy was like Prince Charming. He was oh so cute. He reminded me of what Alex DeLarge would look like if he were real. He wore a suit and was so stern but so inviting. His eyes were captivating. He was the only one who gave me any money—well, let's be honest; he tipped me a hundred just for chatting with him. I tried to be flirty and touch his leg, but he pushed it aside gently and said, "No," that he wasn't going to touch me because he respected me that much. Hello! What? My life is like a book. How fun, right? This diary will be way more interesting than my junior high one, that's for sure. Can't wait to see where this goes. He kissed my hand and got up to leave. He assured me he'd see me again soon.

 No private dances, but it didn't matter. I went home early. Hopefully that was OK? I guess I should've asked, but I was tired. They had plenty of girls anyway. Sure they didn't miss me. Oh, life is a dream. It really is. Who needs school when you look like me?

Love,

T

October 31, 2006

Dear Diary,

Halloween was so fun at the club tonight. I dressed up like Patrick Bateman from American Psycho, complete with chainsaw and white tube socks. Some people really dug it. Stripping really is so easy. I don't know why they get such a bad rap. It's just like in the movies—gorgeous guys, easy money, they can't touch you, pretty girls, designer bags. Oh yeah, that's right. Got my first Coach bag this afternoon before going into work. Such a natural high shopping.

This guy came in who kind of looked like Christian Bale, and he was trying to tempt me to come back to his place for money. Yeah, right, like I would be that girl. Never. He still kept tipping me, trying to touch me. It's so much fun teasing and being a flirt. All these guys want me. Stripping is great for a girl with low self-esteem. You just get to be in charge and then charge that card.

The music was fun tonight too! Love our DJ, Carlos. He's just a fat and happy little thing. He told me if he was a customer, I'd be the girl he'd get a dance with. Maybe he just was saying this for my tip money, but it sure did work. I tipped a hundred considering I made about six hundred tonight. Who'd've thought? Six months ago, I was in a small hillbilly farm town straight out of Deliverance. Six weeks ago, I was under the roof of my father's prison going to boring-ass community college, and now, I'm a real-life video vixen on the Sunset Strip. Life is too good and too easy! Got a big audition in the morning. Got to go to bed. Love my life.

Love,

November 2, 2006

Dear Diary,

He came back! Alex DeLarge came back. Okay, so he's not Alex DeLarge, but his last name is Black. He asked me to call him Mr. Black. Total Reservoir Dogs meets Fifty Shades, but I digress. I got my first present, my first Louboutins ever! I just about died when I saw the red bottoms. I told him I couldn't accept them, but he insisted and said it would be a personal insult if I didn't take them. They looked so good.

He even bought my only dance of the night, a VIP worth five hundred dollars. I started dancing for him, and we ended up slow-kissing. It felt so good. I just wanted him to sweep me off my feet, marry me, and get me pregnant so I'd never have to work again. I just want that more than anything. His kisses were magical. He held my stomach and said one day his baby was going to be inside of there. I just can't stop daydreaming about all this. How did I get so lucky?

The other girls have been pretty nice to me, surprisingly. Probably because I don't make as much as they do, but it doesn't matter. As long as I have money for rent, well, even that doesn't matter because my mom has always offered to help, especially since she just got remarried for the fifth time. It's nice to have that to fall back on.

The club looked beautiful tonight. It was packed, and of course, Mr. Black was there for me. He hasn't asked me for my number yet, which is odd, but I guess he really is trying to be a gentleman.

Love,

T

November 8, 2006

Dear Diary,

Yes! First celebrity came in tonight. It was like a dream! I didn't get a dance from him—I was too shy—but the girls who did were in the back room all night, and on stage, he was "making it rain" (this means just throwing, so many dollar bills in the air it looks like a rainstorm, learning something new every day). I was so enamored by all the pretty girls getting the money. They are so confident on stage. The first month was easy because I was new, but I find myself doubting myself a lot. So not me.

As for me, I got my first "easy paycheck." This guy just paid me to talk to him. I didn't want to stand past midnight since I had already been there all day, but he just kept talking and talking and giving me a twenty for like every twenty minutes that passed just sitting with him on the couch. It was so great, even though the management didn't think so, as I wasn't bringing them any money. I ended up staying till 6:00 a.m., closing time, but it was nice not to have to do anything but listen.

It really reminded me there are a lot of lonely people out there and maybe what I was doing wasn't so bad?

Exotica told me she was making good money going home with some of her clients; she asked me if I wanted to join her tomorrow night. I passed. I don't do that. She does a lot of coke. I don't. I don't think I could get through that. I'm not a prostitute, heck! I'm only doing this for a couple months to make some extra cash, find a new show to be on, anything.

Overall, a good night, pretty uneventful. Exciting to see someone I actually recognized.

Love,

November 20, 2006

Dear Diary,

I almost killed Mr. Black tonight. Ohmygoodness, it was so scary. I knew he was coming in tonight, so I bought new perfume to wear. I felt so good. I hadn't eaten solid foods for a few days, so I knew I looked good. Mr. Black walked in dressed in a gray suit, and I just immediately flushed. I could hardly breathe at how attractive he was. I pretended not to notice so I randomly chatted up some guy at the bar. Mr. Black came over to me and put his hand on the small of my back to lead me into the VIP section of the club. I was confused, scared, embarrassed, and aroused all at once. He must've paid the manager when I was fake talking to the other customer. It was just magical. I felt like I was floating, and in a weird way, I kind of felt like Cinderella, like I was the chosen one. I suppose this was my fucked-up idea of the fairy tale that was meant for me.

As soon as we got in the back, he slowly undressed me, and we had more of the slow kisses. Then he started going down and around my neck, and before he got down to my breasts, he started hacking, coughing so loud I thought my eardrums were going to explode. I was trying to ignore it, but then he stopped and started heavy panting. I asked him what was wrong, and he told me to call an ambulance. I was so scared. The ambulance came, and the paramedics said he'd had an allergic reaction—he was allergic to the perfume I was wearing! Oh no! The three biggest rules of our club I broke tonight. I wore body glitter and perfume, and I called authorities when we are not supposed to (a rule I don't quite understand). I was told to go home and had to surrender my earnings for the night as a penalty. Not fair. Then again, I pretty much work at a brothel, so who am I to report the unfairness to? They need a union for strippers. Mr. Black probably won't be coming back. I think I humiliated him more than I humiliated myself. It wouldn't have worked anyway. A man that *physically perfect was probably just using me to make fun of me or get a giggle, or maybe I was a charity case. Shit. Trish, what is wrong with you?*

Love,
T

December 1, 2006

Dear Diary,

Ohmygosh, why are people so cruel? Why are girls so mean? I can't believe it. My locker was broken into tonight. All my baby wipes are gone! How could this happen? Who steals a whole tub of baby wipes? I just don't understand. What did I do to deserve this? I know it was Heather. She is such a money-hungry, rude, coked-out bitch. She probably stole them for her own baby because she is such a whore.

I had to walk six blocks to get those baby wipes at midnight. I had to endure what seemed like gallons of come on my back with no sanitation wipes. I couldn't wipe my sweat down out of my thighs, I couldn't freshen up my breasts or my underarms. Did Heather want me to smell bad or get a vaginal infection? Is this why she would steal my baby wipes?

What if it wasn't Heather? What if it was Versace or Cherry? Both of those girls have hated me since I've been pulling in more regular clients—their regular clients. Could they be capable of stealing my baby wipes? What if I would've gotten the generic baby wipes? Would that have helped? I'm so confused and hurt and scared. What could be stolen next? What if I got more baby wipes tomorrow? How would I know they'd be safe? I could always put the baby wipes behind the bar, but what if the customers stole them? What if my manager stole them? It's a sad world we live in, when a girl can't be secure about her baby wipes anymore.

Love,

December 16, 2007

Dear Diary,

    I came in to work late tonight, and there was no sign of Mr. Black. He was supposed to be here tonight. He told me he'd be back on this date. I was worried maybe he was in and didn't want to wait for me and left. I can't believe I overslept by two hours. I was so concerned, and I didn't have his number until I saw him. I saw him, and tonight was the first night I've cried since I was a baby. My dad always told me crying was a sign of weakness, and I couldn't believe I was crying in front of all the girls. Of course, they mocked me, but I couldn't help it. Exotica was having sex with Mr. Black in the back room. I wanted to rip her off of him and beat her up, but I realized it wasn't her fault. He was paying to have sex with her. Who wouldn't take that money? That's her job…Why couldn't that have been my job? Was I not pretty enough? Not skinny enough? I went out to sit in the club to wait for more people to come. When he came out of the back room, he had his hands all over Exotica, and she was extremely happy. I overheard her telling another girl he tipped her like ten grand.

    He came over to me, put his hands on me, and started groping me. I told him to fuck off. He asked me what was wrong, and I told him what I saw. His reply was, "I'll get one from you next time if you want, but you weren't here." And that was it. That was all he said. I just couldn't keep from crying. I yelled at him and called him names to which he called me a fat cunt and walked away.

    I couldn't get a dance to save my life tonight. My whole mojo was off. I was reprimanded for leaving early last night so I knew I couldn't get off again. I just felt so low. I still do. Why do guys pretend they like you? Yes, I strip, but I am a human being. Don't play with my emotions. I always do this though. I make relationships more serious than they are in my head. My head is pounding.

Love,
T

December 31, 2006

Dear Diary,

    Spending New Year's Eve in a hospital, which I'll never be able to afford. Fuck. No insurance, no money saved. I did this to myself. Well, I suppose technically it's 2007 now. Pretty sure I'm going to get fired for this one. Mr. Black came back in tonight. I let him sweet-talk me again. It was clear he had no recollection of calling me a "fat cunt" just a few weeks before. He preys on the girls with the low self-esteem, I've noticed. He loves me for the fact that I'll forgive him anything. Even attempted murder tonight.

    I guess he caught wind of our rules and not calling the cops for whatever reasons our managers don't want us to. I'm shaking right now just because I can hardly breathe without this oxygen mask, but for some reason, I'm not shaken up by the fact that neither my managers at the club nor another girl nor Mr. Black himself called the police or an ambulance. To be honest, I don't even know who dropped me off here. I remember it was a good-looking guy, or maybe it was a fat guy. Was it our DJ? I don't know now. All I know is I'm here in this hospital, and my neck is throbbing.

    Mr. Black wanted to tie me up and do choke-out sex tonight. I was a little scared but turned on, I guess. Really the last thing I remember is him undoing my wrists and putting the tie around my neck. I think he was being playful. He was whispering sexy things into my ear. I remember saying, "I can't breathe," and then yelling, "I can't breathe!" Security came back, and then they left. I don't really understand why. Maybe this is in my head, but I swore he said something about my perfume I wore last time, some sort of remark that I was trying to get him but he got me instead. I don't know. I can't keep doing this to myself. Yes, he pays me, but I'm starting to feel I deserve this treatment. I almost wish I would've been choked to death right about now. I know these hospital bills are going straight in the garbage. Fuck. I feel like I was beaten up. Was

I? Would I remember? Doctors think I was raped, asked me where I was tonight. I just said I don't remember. Probably just assume I'm a prostitute. Might as well be.

Love,

T

January 3, 2007

Dear Diary,

Ugh! What a night! Only made fifty dollars on stage and fifty on dances. My beginner's luck has officially worn off. No regulars came in tonight—I hate having to compete with girls who'll do anything for twenty dollars—well, actually, eighteen dollars after tipout...tough, rough. Why am I living in LA again? Oh yeah, I'm going to be the next Marilyn Monroe or something—even I don't remember anymore.

But I ask you...do you think Marilyn subjected herself to eating large amounts of food in front of a chubby chaser while being completely naked? Oh and this was in the fifteen-minute VIP—oh wow. Being desperate is an understatement.

Yes! This guy said he'd been watching me for the past three months (since I started) and was fascinated at my weight loss since last October. Annoyed, I was about to leave until he said he'd get a dance...

Great, worked eight hours and got one lousy dance. He took out Twinkies—I'm not joking—and asked me to suck the filling out and smear the sponge part all over my face. I didn't want to do all that 'cause it's just offensive, but told him I'd do it for an extra twenty dollars. He agreed, but after only one bite, he walked out of the dance and demanded his money back—of course, my manager, being Persian, refused...but I still had to pay a ten-dollar fine at the end of the night. Why? I still don't know.

So, I guess I'm going to take the fifty dollars and invest in some new shoes. Been learning some new pole tricks—still unsure of what I'm doing on stage. Hoping I don't get fired...didn't make much for the club tonight. Oh and nobody appreciated my Buddy Holly set tonight. So tired, going to eat some left-over pizza—maybe that should be part of the stage show...

Love,

T

February 9, 2007

Dear Diary,

What is happening? I can't get a dance to save my life, and my car broke down on the way home tonight. I just left it on the side of the road. I didn't know what to do. Is this a punishment from God? I know I shouldn't be stripping, but why am I always the only one getting punished? Have no idea how I am going to afford to get this fixed when I couldn't even afford my taxi ride home. The taxi driver took my name and address down and told me he'd be back in one week for me to come up with the money. I know I will find someone to borrow it from, but it still leaves me with a sick feeling. On top of that, I haven't paid this month's rent. I don't know what's wrong with me.

I'm always looking for a sign from God. I just don't like that all these signs are trying to detour me from my path to stardom and happiness. Why can't I just be rich? I need more money but what? I don't know how or what. I've had sex before, but the guy never called me back. I couldn't imagine selling sex. I feel terrible for having it with a guy I barely knew, but to get paid for doing that? I guess technically Mr. Black "paid for sex," but I really felt like he loved me and we had a soul connection. And even though I haven't seen him since New Year's Eve, I still feel like he loves me and was just helping me out with the money he gave me. So I don't consider that "money for sex." It just wasn't like that. To have sex with someone you're not in love with—it just sounds like a suicide gateway. If God loved me, he'd give me a good sign that I'm headed in the right direction. It's like, it should only be going up from here. It has to.

Looking at Craigslist for new cars, new jobs. I love going into the adult section to see what people offer. One guy said he'd pay a girl three hundred dollars for one hand job. I emailed him from my fake account to see what he'd say, but he wants to come over to my house. I just couldn't do that, so I stopped and deleted the account.

I'm such a wimp. Story of my life. I need a car. God, please help me fix my car.

Love,

T

March 3, 2007

Dear Diary,

For once, it's early! Home by 9:00 p.m. and what a day…My car is still broken down, and there's still no money to fix it, so I took the bus into work for day shift again.

Day-shift strippers can be divided into two categories—moms and fat chicks—and I'm beginning to think the few customers who trickle in know this…

These fetishists go for the extremely large (e.g., Brooklyn) or the chick who has had so many kids there is no elasticity left in her undercarriage (Sapphire).

Considering I haven't made money these past few days, figured I'd change my strategy to being middle-aged, stuffed, and mopey.

Today was officially my record day as far as day shifts go. Brooklyn and Sapphire had a total of zero dances while Presley had a total of six (including two VIP dances). New engine. Check. New headshots. Check.

To remember for tomorrow and next week: even smaller G-string and no cardio. Also, my two oldest kids I had at fifteen and sixteen, and my middle is from an abandoned sperm. Youngest is only six weeks old. I know, I know, I do look good for just having a baby. Also, Google two blond boys and a mixed infant. Got to save to my phone to show the pictures.

Day shift isn't so bad. It's safer, and I don't have to waste my time talking to the guys. Wish I didn't have to miss auditions. Hopefully car will be up by the end of this month.

Going to take a shower. Period plus dancing equals mess. The cook from next door tried pushing me down onto his lap—big mistake for him, cheap ass. I told him he better wipe that "ketchup" off his crotch before going back to work. Tired. Daytime shift, ninja stripper, out.

Love,

T

May 8, 2007

Dear Diary,

    Tonight is my nineteenth birthday. I celebrated by buying a big sheet cake for myself and taking it into work. All the girls there are calling me anorexic, so I wanted them to see it. Truth be told, I'm on a sort of cleanse. I've been cleansing my body for the past six weeks, down to about 120 pounds but still think i'm too fat. I posted a video on YouTube before coming to work tonight. It was my warm-up, dancing to a song from the Reservoir Dogs soundtrack! I guess one of the girls found my YouTube channel. She actually thought it was pretty cool even though she said my apartment looked like a dump, which it is.

    My manager found out it was my birthday. I'm thinking he knew from Myspace even though we're not friends. He was very sweet, brought me some vodka. I know that may not seem like a sweet gesture, but for him, it was. I met the sweetest gentleman tonight too. He said his name was Rodd Thunder, sounded like a fake name, but heck, I said my name was Presley. He was really fascinated by my name choice. He talked about loving Elvis as a boy. He blushed a lot too. It was cute. Showed me pictures of his thirteen-year-old daughter, and I just smiled, knowing a father could love his daughter so much and be so proud that he'd even show a stripper a picture of her. I could tell he loved her, said he hustled for her. I joked that he was a drug dealer. He said I was close. He was an actor. He did look semi-familiar, I suppose. He said I was pretty and that he was probably too old for me. I could've played into that, played him, but I had a weird amount of respect for him, so much so I didn't even ask for a dance. He asked if it would be inappropriate to exchange email addresses. I gave him mine. He was also the first person I told my real name to in the club. He was very handsome. He just made me smile and got me giddy for some reason. I told him it was my birthday, and he was sorry I was working. I said I didn't mind because I don't know that many people.

Not much exciting after that. Ate my whole cake and split the vodka with some of the girls. As I was getting ready to leave, my manager walked in with a beautiful bouquet of roses that looked like something a big movie star would receive after winning an Oscar. No Oscar. They were from "Rodd." I'd never gotten anything so spectacular in all my life. And tonight, these long-stem roses were better than any money or dance sold. These were a kind gesture just for some conversation. It touched my heart.

Back to dieting tomorrow. I don't think anyone would've bought me such flowers twenty pounds ago. Wish I would've talked to my dad or my mom tonight. I miss them. I'm sure they want nothing to do with me. That's OK. Rodd felt a lot like my father actually. It felt good.

Love,

T

June 2, 2007

Dear Diary,

    Feeling weaker and weaker as these weeks go by. About to take a few months off from dancing to go shoot this reality TV show for the ScyFy network. Trying to lose another twenty pounds before I get on TV. I feel so blessed because dancing is draining me. I feel like this might be my "big break." Finally got to talk to my mom today. She's on her fifth marriage but looks like it's going south. What else is new? I also talked to my father tonight. He came into the club. Well, not my real father, of course. Rodd. We've been email buddies. He's never asked me out, nor has he been back in the club since my birthday. I can't tell if he's shy or if he's married. I try not to pry. I just enjoy having him for conversation via email. I get lonely. I think he gets lonely too. He's starting a play in New York this fall on Broadway. It's pretty exciting. Still not sure if Rodd Thunder is his real name. I don't think so. I Googled him, and, of course, everything and nothing came up. Not in the actor field anyway. I don't know why he'd lie to me.

    He told me I was looking very thin and asked if I was OK. He even offered me money. I told him to keep it for his daughter and that I still have those roses he sent to the club for me all dried up and used as a bookmark. He still was a little uneasy about his age. I assured him he didn't look a day over thirty, which is the truth. He told me he had just turned fifty. I was shocked.

    Tonight was pretty lucrative, but I think aside from money and good company, I also was getting a strong sign from God that tonight was going to be my last night ever to work as a stripper. My neighbor Eddie, who was a child actor, asked me to move in with him, split the bills. That's going to save us both a lot. We have sex on the casual, but I see him more as a friend. Also with the reality show I just booked, Rodd as a nice guy, and these girls who came in to reach out to us, I feel like God really is putting me on a better path. These girls came from the sex industry in some form or another, and they try to help other girls get out as well. They come in as sexy clothes salesgirls, but they really just try to talk to us to get us out of there. One of the girls warned me that stripping was a gateway to prostitution. I told her, "This is all temporary for me. I'm clean, straight edge, and just booked a huge TV job." She said she prayed this would be my last night and she said I needed to too. I felt so much compassion from her without ever knowing her. I really felt she was a godsend to me, reassuring me everything is going to be OK.

Love,

T

October 4, 2007

Dear Diary,

Thank goodness, the strip club took me back. The show was a complete bomb. I was eliminated after six days of being in that house. Why do I keep thinking I'm better than I am? Why do I keep thinking I can do this whole Hollywood thing when I clearly cannot? The constant struggle, I haven't eaten in months and still no one will hire me. It doesn't matter. I ordered a pizza all to myself tonight at the club and got McDonald's on the way home. Food never fails me. Food doesn't ignore my emails like Rodd. Food doesn't kick me out of my own house for drugs like Eddie. Food doesn't try to take control over me like my father. And food doesn't make me feel bad about myself; it makes me happy. The only constant in my life is food. I love food.

Food is the way for me. I got a guy who told me if I gained about forty pounds, I'd be the hottest thing in the world to him, that he'd marry me so fast if I gained a potbelly and some booty. I told him I would, just for him. I will. He was super cute too. I don't know what he did, and I didn't care. He got a dance and told me he couldn't wait to watch and feel my belly grow, that he'd come in week after week to see my progress. He tipped me a couple hundred for food and beer. He said beer bellies were the sexiest thing on a woman. I love him. No more pressure to be skinny. I'm at a dirty club for the rest of my life. I might as well eat and be happy about it. Food is so good.

I worship food. I just want to eat food all day long. I'll work dayshift again if I have to. I don't care. I like my nights free anyway. It allows me to create more YouTube videos. The Internet is such a wonderful place. I love it. Not as much as I love food, but I love it. Going to sleep so well tonight.

Love,

T

October 10, 2007

Dear Diary,

Brian took me out on a date tonight to Hamburger Hamlet before work. I told him about my plans to get fat, and he laughed. He told me I'd be beautiful no matter what. Brian is so sweet to me. He takes me out. We watch TV, and we laugh. I can spend the whole night with Brian, and we'll never have sex. He's such a gentleman to me. I haven't seen him in so long. He asked me how I liked stripping. I told him he had to come in, which he's only done once. He dropped me off but didn't even come in. I told him I'd dance to his boss's music tonight. He said he hears it enough. Maybe he's not really attracted to me in that way. I'm OK with that. I'm not attracted to him at all either, but it's always nice to feel adored.

I danced to classic rock the whole night. We had a few classic rock stars stop by, one of whom is famous for being married to his high school sweetheart and being so loyal to her. I didn't talk to him, but I know the girls he got dances from—loyal my ass. Spoke with Brian a few minutes ago, and he said he knows that guy is the biggest manwhore of them all. He asked me if I slept with him. I just rolled my eyes, and he knew I was rolling my eyes at him even over the phone! So funny, right?

There were also rumors tonight that this girl who went by the name Feline was abducted last night from the club. Kind of gives me the chills thinking about it. I told Brian if that ever happened to me, it was his fault. I was joking, but he took it so seriously. I just need lots of prayers right now, and I pray for her safe return. I never really talked with her before, but no one deserves that.

So exhausted, Brian said we're going out for a big breakfast before work tomorrow so I can be nice and fat for all my chubby-chasing men. Love him. Good night.

Love,

T

October 16, 2007

Dear Diary,

    I've been dancing officially for a year now (still waiting on that big break) and was hoping for a low-key night at work. Had to go in early 'cause my manager texted that the doctor was in and was waiting for me. I got there and gave him his dance, four for forty dollars—the usual; he mentioned something about the new tube socks I was wearing. Didn't think much of it until later on in the night when the DJ called Presley to the bar again (which, PS, I'm regretting that name because this club is such a piece of trash, Elvis should not have to be associated with it). I digress...

    So this new manager tells me the doctor wants a one-hour VIP with me! Why? I didn't know—he knows I'm not a dirty dancer...but whatever, maybe he was drunk? Nope. He was sober. Omg. Diary! He wanted me to give him my socks for five hundred dollars! So I did, and for another five hundred he wanted to eat my feet while I put the sweaty socks in my mouth! Was this worth a thousand dollars? No! I'm so sick to my stomach. What kind of diseases can I get from foot/mouth contact? Seriously, I need my prayer book. I need to get out of stripping; I've officially degraded myself as low as you can go. Oh! I don't want to be punished! Don't punish me, God. I'm a good person with a good heart and a clean conscience and an even cleaner body. What do I do? I should never have bought that new car—these payments are making me crazy. And now my poor doughnut socks are with a creepy creeperson. Officially the lowest. How am I supposed to go in tomorrow? Oh and I already threw those shoes in the dumpster. Left early and told the manager, I quit! (again)...

Love,

T

October 19, 2007

Dear Diary,

    Brian came in today! He came in and got dances with every girl but me. I yelled at him inside the club, told him to rot in hell. He looked like he was about to cry. I told him never to call me and to lose my number. Why would he do this to me? He is someone I talk to day in and day out. I share all my stories with him...He was the one who convinced me to strip in the first place, for the money. I go out with him, his ugly face and my pretty face, and he's not going to even get a dance for me? He didn't yell back. He just left. I was so mad. I still am so mad. Why are guys always trying to hurt me?

    I told a bunch of lies to get dances tonight. Told guys whatever they wanted to hear just to get them in the back room and to make myself feel better. Of course, guys walked out as soon as I wouldn't fuck them or sit on their dirty laps for that matter. I just wanted to be wanted, wanted to feel love, whatever that is.

    Worked on stage a lot. Think I twisted my ankle. My manager thought I was drunk, which I wasn't. I really can't be in our club. They make it impossible for anyone to smuggle alcohol in. My manager also hinted that the club was a cover-up for a drug den. I told him I was going to expose him if he ever fired me. He told me not to make threats, blah blah blah. He asked me if I knew pain, I told him to fuck off. I'm done with guys trying to intimidate me.

Love,

T

November 11, 2007

Dear Diary,

What is with guys? I mean seriously—are all guys born without half of their brain...or just the ones who come into strip clubs?

OK, so this guy named Gary came in. I decided to not tell him I was semi-new but rather make him feel as though I was a pro and worth the money (guys don't like desperate and sad, I've found out). Gary was so polite to me; he looked at me in my eyes while we talked, conversed with me about his life as a professor at a very prestigious college, his goals, my goals, and so on. He kept going on and on and on about how my hair was beautiful, my smile was kind, and how I was radiating the room. Typically, a guy that sweet and that cute would not want a dance—the "newbie Presley" in me would've just said "nice to meet you and bye"...but since I was trying to be "Presley, pole-dance pussycat extraordinaire," I pushed for the dance...

Assuming he'd be polite and just get the typical four for forty dollars was only the beginning of my error in judgment. He went for the fifteen-minute VIP for $120—in the back! I only did this once on my second night and did it so wrong, the guy asked for his money back. But I wasn't worried about that with Mr. Polite. Gary had a daughter after all.

The DJ announced the VIP beginning, and instantly, Gary pulled me down on his lap and pulled my hair back so hard my extensions loosened and my head followed. I thought, *This is it; I'm a dirty stripper whore, and I will now die a stripper whore death.* Oh much worse—Gary turned into G$, and he said for a hundred dollars more, all I had to do was call him...ohmygoodness..."daddy." So I did. I had to endure grinding on a nonexistent you-know-what for the next fourteen minutes while he amused himself with such intellectual quips as "You're daddy's naughty little girl" and "Daddy's got a present for his nasty little slut."

After the dance, Gary shook my hand, thanked me, and said he'd be in next week and went to the bathroom. What a prince.

Love,

T

November 18, 2007

Dear Diary,

    My manager, Vic, told me some disturbing news today. Apparently, he needs another copy of my license because mine was in his bookbag, which was allegedly "stolen" and had about thirty grand in cash inside. I was a little confused and very scared. Who had my address and license now? A little disheartening.

    Tonight was my first night holding drugs. Vic asked me to put them in my purse until he asked for them, but he went home early. Now I have all these little baggies in my purse, praying nobody will find them. My phone keeps ringing, but it's from an unknown number, and when I answer, it's just silence. One of the girls told me to be careful with Vic. He is flirty, but I think it's pretty harmless. He's good-looking for a Persian guy. I don't know. He seems nice, just trying to keep on everyone's good side.

    Side note, another chubby chaser came in today. I'm like 140 pounds. Is this chubby? I guess maybe. We also had a girl start today who's real age is sixteen. Goodness, I don't know who let her slip in, but she really is a baby, a cracked-out baby, but a baby no less. Kind of itchy, hoping no bedbugs came home with me. So paranoid about that for some reason. Oh God, phone is ringing again. So weird, this whole night has been weird to say the least. Definitely need some sleep. There's a Bill Murray marathon on TV right now. Bill Murray was my dad's neighbor for the longest time, and for some reason, I find myself fantasizing about him coming into the strip club and getting a lap dance from me. It's weird, especially since he goes to my church. Who doesn't love Bill Murray?

                                             Love,

                                                 T

December 4, 2007

Dear Diary,

Went to the ER tonight. Cannot say anymore. I just pray to God for one miracle—that I'll be able to walk again. I made some wrong decisions. I talked to the wrong people. I'm damaged goods. What if I can't dance again? What if I can't walk again?

They did the tests on me tonight; they know. But I can't tell who or why. The police told me if I didn't tell them anything, there was nothing I could do, and the abusers would be walking around free and potentially could do this again to me or another girl.

Too scared. Too scared to talk to them, to even write. My life is too precious to me. Right now, in this moment, I just want to live. I promise to be good. I just want to live. My heart is in the right place. I just want to have another chance.

Girls shouldn't be scared to talk. When will the authorities do more than just hand out restraining orders that are easily broken. Anymore, a person has to attempt to kill you before anything gets attention. It's just not that easy to name names without any protection, much less without a doorknob to my apartment.

I'm officially that girl. That girl who sits in silence. Who lives her life in fear. I'm forever living a life of fear from here on out. My innocence is no more. I don't trust this world. I only trust God...as of now.

Love,

T

December 25, 2007

Dear Diary,

I am quitting! Quitting dancing forever! No more will I put up with finger slips or tongue slips or liars or cheaters or construction workers who never shower! And above all else, no crazy management who beats up girls! Its Christmas Day—I can't afford to go back home and see my family. I'm stuck working a double shift at the worst strip club ever, and there are bruises all over my legs from the pole and now two matching ones on my eye and lip! The worst part is I can't even go to the cops because the managers and owners are so shady and are always threatening me. Got a new phone on a new carrier and have enough saved up to figure out what I'm going to do next.

I'm not a slut. I don't deserve this. Although if I was, this wouldn't have happened and I'd have a whole lot more saved up by now. Really worrying about my face. It's like throbbing. Think I'm going to have to break down and call my father...just so lost and don't know what else to do. I know I got to regroup and get myself together. What if I permanently damaged my face? Hoping the physical me will heal but praying for the emotional me to be restored. This life I'm living is no life at all...My tires were shot. I'm just glad it wasn't me. I spiraled into this hole. Time to dig myself back out...I will not be defeated! I'm so much better than this...

The bleeding won't stop...flashes of fists and guns coming at me, haunting me—they have my license and my address, praying there won't be a repeat of what happened. I am still alive, but Presley is officially dead!

Love,

T

December 31, 2007

Dear Diary,

Do strippers deserve to be raped? Is it part of our job? Is it rape if you tease? I'm numb. I started a different type of diary tonight, a prayer journal. I need Christ more than ever. I feel like after the incident, I lost who I was. I am still lost. I'm searching every day. I can't even leave my house. I haven't slept in days since it happened. In fact, I'm scared they know where I live. They might kill me if they think I'm going to talk. I wouldn't. I couldn't. I'm too scared. It's too scary. I probably deserved it.

I can't stop crying right now, literally sobbing. How often does this happen? Why did this happen to me? How many more girls will this happen to? Honestly, I'm scared to have children in this world. It's such an unfair and cruel world. I'm shaking and peeing in my living room. I'm scared someone is behind my shower curtain. New Year's Eve will be my death. Will it be '07 or '08? Maybe '09 if I make it that far.

I don't know what I look like. My neighbor, Superman, and his wife keep coming to check on me. I scream at the door like a banshee. Haven't talked to my family in months. Wonder what they would think of me? They'd probably be happy they were right about me all along, that I am actually a screw-up.

God, just take me whenever you want me. God, point me in the path you want me if that be on this earth or if that be with you.

Love,

January 14, 2008

Dear Diary,

New year, new club, new Trish, or whoever I want to be. Yesterday, I started at this club in Hollywood. It's prestige, and I was shocked I even got hired. These girls were definitely hard to compete with—beautiful faces, perfect bodies, and graceful movement. How was I going to compete? Easy. That was the answer. I was going to be easy.

The first celebrity face I recognized, I went up, introduced myself, massaged his inner thigh, and said he could have all of me if he got the full-hour VIP in the back. He went with me; he didn't even look at any of the girls. He walked in and sat down for exactly one minute before I pounced. Is it bad to say I was proud of myself? Forget Presley—heck, forget Trish—it was all about Ten (which I told guys was short for Tennessee, just a little dirty Southern vixen, don't you see?).

I gave him just enough to want more. He asked when I worked again and what a thousand dollars could get him? I told him, "Why don't we find out tomorrow (today) outside of the club?"

This is exciting, going to an actual movie star's house. I feel just like Julia Roberts in Pretty Woman. Will I get beaten up like last year? Maybe. But at least I'll go down in infamy, maybe even get an E! True Hollywood Story.

So nervous but excited, hoping maybe he'll ask me to marry him and take me away from all this. Who knows? Either way, I am going to get laid and paid. Patting myself on the back.

Love,
T

January 29, 2008

Dear Diary,

    Worked the day shift today, with a bunch of fatties. I loved this girl Pearl though. She is a sweet woman, definitely past her prime, but she sat down and gave me some motivational speech today. It touched my heart. She said that she knew I was escorting, but she wasn't going to say anything nor was she going to charge me. She just told me to make that money while my skin is still tight and the money is still right. I opened up to her about my mom for some reason, and she said, "It's all going to work out, baby." I told her I thought about writing a story or doing a video about what it's really like to be a stripper. She told me not to leave her out of it and that if it ever got made into a TV movie, that she got to play herself, if she was alive. I laughed, but sadly, I think she was being serious. Pearl has her regular customers, and she has a good spirit.

    We had a director come in during the day. He was looking for a date for his premier that night at Grauman's. I thought he was full of shit, but I played along with him. Truth was, he actually did have a movie premiere. He offered me a grand for the screening and extra if the evening went that way. I said, "Sure, why not?" What did I have to lose? Guess who was the star of this movie? Rodd Thunder! Well, in fact, Rodd Thunder wasn't his name at all, like I figured. I just about died. I kept having to run into the bathroom and dodge him. I don't think my date even noticed. I had a feeling I was more there for the "evening went that way" part, so I was off the hook. "Rodd" looked amazing on the screen. There is something so warm and charming about him, no matter what part he's playing. He's very captivating, and I found myself daydreaming about him throughout the rest of that night's events. The director was nice, came fast, paid in cash, and then told me he had to get up early tomorrow. That's a bunch of bullshit. He told me not to say anything, super paranoid. I told him I didn't give a shit about him. I really didn't. He was a lame lay, but that's the sad part about most of these Hollywood hotshots: they have to make lots of money to compensate for their lack of sexual skills. Jewish, no less. I told him I had Jesus in my life, and he looked a little freaked. He didn't even ask if I needed money for a taxi ride home, even though I was hammered. What a prince.

Pearl just texted me a few minutes ago, told me to call her if I needed anything. So sweet. She told me I had more going for me than I realized. I don't know why her words resonate so much with me, almost like it's another sign from God. Maybe I'm just misinterpreting these signs wrong. Maybe Rodd was a sign that I need to call my father. I don't know, trying to make sense of it all. Made two boxes of mac and cheese, not even going to shower. This Jewish come makes my vagina feel refreshed.

Love,

T

February 5, 2008

Dear Diary,

    I'm starting to have my own sadistic thoughts. Am I becoming crazy? I know I wasn't born crazy, but I'm thinking I should go see a shrink. Every night at the club, I have visions of my stripper heel hooking a guy's eye out. I have thoughts of my panties being razor sharp and slowly tracing their faces only to carve an outline for their entire face to fall off. These aren't normal, I know, but it's scary. I even dream at night about going back to my old club and just setting the place on fire or driving my car through the front and just knocking it down.

    Tonight, as I was talking to this customer, he was telling me all the dirty things he wanted to do with me. I slipped into a Patrick Bateman moment, where I just was having my own conversation in my head. He'd say things like "How would you like my hot sausage inside of your tight little hole?" and my mental response was "How would you like a hot little black mamba placed inside your intestines and have only your penis head hole as an escape, by pushing through and biting the tip?"

    I have problems. God, please help me. I know I am going through these financial struggles and physical health problems, but these mental fights are killing me. Slowly but surely. God, show me the way. I pray for the day when I can share my testimony with girls going through the same thing, my story of redemption. Mental illness is scary. I've been reading so much about it online, but I know God is capable of healing and being a miracle worker. Prayer is my best medicine right now.

Love,

February 14, 2008

Dear Diary,

Its Valentine's Day, and I had three "dates" tonight. I told each of them they got one hour with me and that was it and that the thousand dollars had to be in cash. One motherfucker tried to write me a check. I didn't care who he was; I made him go to an ATM to get it out.

The first guy was very sweet; he was an average guy who did accounting or something? Little penis, didn't care.

Second date was an actor from back in the day. He tried to impress me with all his memorabilia. Double wrapped his penis, didn't care.

Third date was the one. I've been a huge fan of this guy's show for a while now. I was excited. He didn't want to wear a condom. I begged him to, but alas, he just went ahead and did it without. He tipped me an extra five thousand—I assume to keep my mouth shut. I told him I wasn't on birth control, and he just laughed. He actually did talk to me for a little bit after sex. I asked him why he had to pay for sex. He told me he doesn't pay for sex; he pays for me to leave. Point taken. I left.

Guys are assholes. They just are. I'm done with this escorting on the side. It makes me feel really lonely and empty. I sort of feel like this is all wrong, but I don't know how to stop. Figure it out later. Going to bed.

Love,

T

February 26, 2008

Dear Diary,

    Ready for this one? I was on second stage tonight, and this new chick went up on the main stage at the same time. She was definitely hot and doing all these crazy tricks. She did this one where she put her head in the guy's crotch on the chair and flipped over, so her crotch was in his face and legs in the air…It was pretty amazing until she shit her pants! This chick actually started anal leaking through her G-string, and you could smell it bad. The guy pushed her off, and she fell on her neck. Surprised she didn't break it. She had to be high, as she was laughing about the whole thing. She came back to the dressing room and said she and her boyfriend had anal sex for the first time earlier in the day and it just kept coming out. The manager wouldn't even let her leave.

    I was in a lap dance when I heard she did the exact same thing—on stage this time. And it was all over the stage. The club had to eventually close early to clean up the mess and the stench. Read some reviews online about it, sad to say, but I think this will actually help this club's reputation. A lot of the guys online were commenting how they are into that shit, pun intended. It was great. Pretty sure she'll be fired or fined at the very least. Also heard she was banging our manager, so maybe she'll still be there.

    Like is this real life? I seriously feel like I'm in a movie, like the movie of my life has to include this chick pooping all over these guys. Strippers are without a doubt the most disgusting creatures to walk this earth. That's not a myth or a stereotype or a judgment; that's just the truth.

Love,

T

February 28, 2008

Dear Diary,

    I'm a lesbian motherfucker. I'm a little girl in a petticoat. I dream of riding carousels all night long. I was on a carousel tonight on stage. William Shakespeare would be so proud of me; I just know he would. He would tell me I was his inspiration. I am his inspiration. Everyone knows he was writing about me; I could sense it.

    That's when the dogs started chasing me. The dogs came into the club, but I'm not sure how they got in there. I suspect it was ol' Doc Brown from the general store. I got to get out of Dodge, but they won't let me. Why won't they let me, Ma? Why can't I just be a normal gal? I don't ask for much. I just want to stare at the stars; that wouldn't hurt anyone, would it?

    Come get me, Papa. Papa is going to come get me. He told me he was coming back for me. I was an angel from above on that stage tonight. They called me an angel. Angel actually got pissed though. Those were her dances, she said.

    I'm not a Smurf, but you are. I'm not a cat, but you are. Why do you insist on this nonsense? Do you hear me, Brutus? Cassius, do you hear me? Let's teach that in English class, Mister Know-it-all. You hear me now? You hear me now, don't you? Come eat some burritos with me, baby. That's all I want.

    They want tits and ass. That's what I give them. You think I'm a stripper whore? You're wrong. You're all wrong. Don't tell me I'm weird unless you're Crispin Glover. Bill Murray gets me. Bill Murray fucking gets everyone; that's why he's going to be president one day.

Love,

T

March 10, 2008

Dear Diary,

God is good. I had a Christian man come into the strip club today. He was another pay-to-talk kind of guy. He told me he was a Christian inspirational speaker. He was a good talker, I'll give him that. He told me God created me for a reason and that he could just tell I was destined for great things. He told me one day God is going to provide for me a platform from which to speak to people, whether that be a couple people or a couple thousand people, and when that time comes, I need to preach the word of the Lord.

I told him I believed in God, I never lost sight of him, and that he was always there for me. I also told him about some of my demons, mental demons, and my side-job demons. He told me they were tests, and God is going to give me strength to overcome, I just have to keep praying. I told him I tried to when I remember to pray, and he said that wasn't enough. He told me to pray when things are going good, when they're going bad, when I have everything, and when I have nothing, when times are slow, when things get quiet, just pray, and pray often.

I couldn't go around to anyone after he left. I felt a little sick. Prayed I wasn't pregnant. Then I realized, I was praying for the wrong things. Instead of praying I was not pregnant, I realized now I needed to pray that I was going in the direction God wanted for me. I prayed that he understood why I was doing the things I was doing, even though I couldn't understand them myself.

Made no money today, but even though my bank account didn't grow, my faith did. I feel stronger. I'm not expecting a miracle overnight, but I pray that in time, God's plan will be revealed.

Love,

June 2, 2008

Dear Diary,

Tonight at work, I couldn't stop itching. I know a lot of the girls said that this club had bedbugs and not to sit on the couches. I'm so worried. I'm still so itchy in between my legs, and it's painful when I urinate.

Guys still try and touch in the private dance rooms. Do they not care what they get? Are they just that horny?

I had one guy try to slip his penis in me while I was just grinding with my face away from him. I screamed and ran out. This manager kind of reminded me of Bill Murray. He just started and was pretty funny most of the time, but he grabbed me and said, "You go back in and finish the dance." I told him what had happened, and he laughed. Why are guys always laughing at me? It's not going to be so funny when I come back and expose you all.

I went back in and stood there. The guy smacked my face and called me a whore. I told him to fuck off and spit in his face. When the manager heard this, he fired me.

Great, another strip club down. Now what am I supposed to do, quit? Going to the free clinic tomorrow, a little nervous, never had an STD test before. Ugh, this is obnoxious. I kind of just want to cry. I hate being stressed out.

Love,

T

July 4, 2008

Dear Diary,

Going into work and feeling so low. Lost about thirty pounds this past month. I'm back with Eddie. He's doing a TV show now, so hopefully it'll take off and I can quit for good.

Went into the club early tonight. Brooklyn was shooting up. I never tried drugs before, but with the condition my body is in anyway, I might as well try. It felt good. I didn't feel anything. I don't even remember the night, but I did come home with about three thousand in cash, and that felt pretty good. Eddie wondered how I made it. I was honest and told him, I didn't know.

Writing this now, I feel a little woozy. Don't know why. My body is officially broken. I'm a broken woman at twenty years old. This is awesome. A guy asked me about being a submissive tonight. Had to Google that one. Don't think I'm that fucked up…not yet anyway. Though I suppose I am somewhat experienced, thanks to Mr. Black almost trying to kill me. I still think about him from time to time. Then again, I think about all the guys I have loved so far from time to time. Wow. I didn't realize this is how my body would react to drugs, wow. Is it a spasm or a convulsion I'm feeling? Is it a trip? I'll be surprised if I make it to twenty-one but hey! Shit! Happens! If you can't be famous, might as well be infamous, right?

Eddie doesn't believe in God. I believe in God. I also believe God hates me or is punishing me for a past life. Day in, day out, here I go. Going back in tomorrow. Working seven days a week to support both of us kind of sucks…

Going to a convention this week, hoping to make some cash there. My hair is so gross.

Love,

July 6, 2008

Dear Diary,

Gene Wilder came in today. No, no, he didn't. Willy Wonka came in today. Willy Wonka asked for a lap dance. Willy Wonka paid me in golden tickets. I have so many golden tickets right now. Eddie fed me an Everlasting Gobstopper while I was dancing for Willy Wonka. I think of my Willy Wonka as Gene Wilder. Gene Wilder would love me; I know he would. Mel Brooks would date me. Mel Brooks and Bill Murray walk into a strip club...

No, I don't think they ever would. I've got the golden ticket. I've got it. Wait till I tell my grandpa. Shit, both of my grandpas are dead. Fuck. Why? Why wasn't I closer with my grandfathers? Why am I not closer with my dad? Why doesn't Bill Murray love me?

If I become famous, I will tell the stories of Willy Wonka's willy inside of me tonight. Nope. We did coke. I can't talk about that. Nope. Eddie said I write too much, I think too much. He said I'm not made for thinking. He's not made for thinking. He's just jealous of me and Willy Wonka. He's just jealous Willy Wonka shared his goodies with me tonight and not him, but I shared my goodies with Eddie. I always share my goodies with him. He doesn't supply; I do. Why? Because I am the supplier. I am the candyman! Fuck Sammy Davis, I am the candyman. I am the candyman! I am the candyman, got it? Got that, Willy Wonka? I am the candyman, the motherfucking candyman.

Love,

T

July 7, 2008

Dear Diary,

Comic Con went great in Long Beach, so much fun, renewed sense of what I'm doing out here in LA. Met an actor who goes by Michael, made my heart flutter. Left Eddie's ass today and spent the whole day with Michael before going into work. He said he loves me, and I love him. So excited. He has such a beautiful place by the beach. This is it. This will be my life, and he is OK with me being a stripper.

Tonight was my last trick, no more escorting. I am finally deeply truly in love. So excited, and Michael is Catholic like me. This guy at work was so gross. I literally had to do two lines before doing the dance. I guess we had sex. I can't remember, but I don't like that. I like to be in control of my mind and body, especially with Michael. Told Michael about this director who came in, he told me to call him next time he does. Everyone loves this guy because he really is a brilliant moviemaker. Why's he at a strip club? I don't know? Seems like he could get laid. I don't know. It's bizarre.

Writing this from Michael's bed. Oh my goodness, am I so happy! Shooting for a show next week about my "tanning addiction." Really, I would've made up any addiction for five hundred dollars, whatever. I'm looking to get out of the strip club so Michael respects me even more. Things are looking up.

Love,

T

August 3, 2008

Dear Diary,

    Michael sent me roses to the club tonight. Oh goodness, I'm such a lucky girl. When I got home, he had a hot plate of food from my favorite Chinese restaurant waiting for me, and when I got upstairs after my shower, he was up waiting for me watching television. He held me like a little girl, and I just broke down and told him I hated what I was doing. He told me I could quit whenever I wanted, that he would be there for me. He was always going to be there for me.

    I told him about the dances and that I couldn't make money by playing clean. I was battling over it because I love him so much I feel like it's cheating. He told me it's all going to be OK. He asked me if any men touched me, and I told him they did but I didn't want it. He told me to get in the bathtub, and he began to clean me. He told me he was going to take care of me like this forever.

    When I got out, we made love, not more than a few minutes ago. He passed out quickly after that. I have such a love for him. I feel like this is the father I've always wanted, the father I've always needed. He cared about me regardless of what I was doing.

    Truth be told, I don't know what rape is anymore. If you don't want guys touching on you or in you, but they do it anyway, is that rape? I feel violated. I do. I get scared when guys want to touch me, I get scared of guys, but for some reason, I'm safe with Michael. He gets me.

    Girls saw what had happened tonight, and they saw that I wasn't affected by it. What does this mean? I barely made a few hundred bucks, and I feel like I could just die. I probably would if I didn't have Michael. It's more than just wanting him. I need him. I need him more than the air I breathe.

Love,

T

October 31, 2008

Dear Diary,

    I'm back in my own apartment tonight. Tonight is the first night I've come home from work and can't be with Michael. He's in NYC for some family thing, and I'm devastated. He texts me every hour though, and that's second best, knowing I'm always on his mind and he's on mine. We are truly soul mates. I hate it when he questions what I do at the club though. He was a little drunk when we talked just now and told me I was a whore. I know he loves me, but I really hate that word. I just want him back here, and everything will be fine.

    Halloween at strip clubs is the most fascinating thing to me. I was dressed as Ronald Reagan and got more dances without trying than ever before. What does this say about men? You know how men always want to do anal sex with a girl, but it's like why? Why not find a gay man to do that with? Well, here's my theory: all men are a little gay. I was in a dress shirt and tie and jacket tonight and made ten times what I've been making wearing a G-string and pasties. They were turned on by the suit with no pants?

    I tied up this one guy who came in with his girl. I tied his hands behind his back while I sat on top of him and his girl sat on top of me. His erection came in 2.4 seconds. He asked me to call him a sissy. I did. Then he asked me to demean him in front of his chick, and I did—and I liked it. It felt so good. Between the suit and the verbal abuse, it was the closest I've ever felt to having balls. It was fun. Does that make me sick? Probably. I'm sick in the head; it's nothing new.

    Just happy to come home to the normalcy that is my love, my Michael. What would I do without him? Pretty sure I would be institutionalized by now. Just a few more days…

Love,

November 2, 2008

Dear Diary,

Michael is a cheater! He fucking cheated. Guys are fucking dumb. When I called him after seeing his domestic thing in the news, he blamed it on me, using the stripper card. Whatever, so done with him. He is an eighties loser has-been anyway. At least Eddie was up front about his bullshit. Michael is a lying douchebag.

Went back to the club tonight. Did a few bumps, and now I'm feeling spacey. My manager asked me out again, like what the fuck? Why do I want to go out with him? I don't. He's an asshole too. All guys are assholes.

I grinded on a lot of dudes tonight, and some motherfucker shot his fucking come on my back. I elbowed him in the face, and he dropped his cash. You're not allowed to pull out your penis, so I didn't get in trouble for hitting him. I kept all nine hundred dollars that dropped out, and I did not feel bad. I am not a come dumpster, asshole.

All men are pigs. All men are scum. This other dude, Mexican construction worker, these are the worst. They whistle at you to come over. He put his finger inside me while I was on stage. I've seen him before, and if he does that again, I will literally hurt him.

Don't trust men; they are fucking snakes.

Love,

T

November 16, 2008

Dear Diary,

    Not sure what happened tonight. It's as if I didn't live in my body tonight. All I know is, I was almost arrested but not sure what for. My manager slapped me, and that's when I came to. He told me he was going to call the cops if I didn't blow him? I was confused. I am confused. I think that's what happened.

    My mom is upset at me. Funny thing, at twenty years old, my mom living thousands of miles away from me, and yet she can still make me feel so small. Again, not sure how she got involved. I know she said something about wiring money to someone. I don't know. I guess this is what she gets for fucking all those guys on the couch while I was sleeping in the next room. Her running naked in our house when I was just a kid set the bar. So I don't feel bad. I do feel bad, but I'm not sure why.

    My heels are fucking broken. Shit. I have no money for this shit. My nails broke too—well, at least like three of them. I think I saw the dude from that movie tonight. I don't know.

    I can't have sex with my manager. Did I have sex with my manager? I don't even know anymore. Really, what is sex? Sex is sex. It's like shaking hands. I shake hands every day. I think I still have a job. Eating some ice cream to soothe my crotch. In fact, I'm going to put this ice cream on my crotch. Ah, that feels so good. So soothing.

                                      Love,

                                          T

November 28, 2008

Dear Diary,

So this dude I did a TV show with, found him on Facebook, and he obviously wants to bang me. I'm not an idiot anymore: you want to bang me; you come into the club. He did.

So this guy is a comedian. He does mostly stand-up now, but he used to do some pretty major films. He comes in with his sunglasses and laptop and little white boy jacket. I think all the other strippers were jealous. He got a dance in the back. I think he was shocked when I actually went down on him, and then we had sex. He was so paranoid after about the cameras. Even tonight, he texted me about the cameras and asked if I was sure they didn't work. How would I know if they didn't? He had his sunglasses on anyway, like it would matter. Apparently, he has a girlfriend, told me to tell her nothing happened. Whatever, used to lying. He's straight though, no drugs.

Still thinking about Michael even after all this fucked-up shit. I don't deserve to be in love. Relationship karma will forever be around to bite me in the ass. I probably fucked up a lot of marriages and fucked over a lot of guys.

Feeling nauseous. Going to lie down.

Love,

T

December 1, 2008

Dear Diary,

    Feeling nauseous. One girl thinks I'm pregnant because I keep throwing up. I hope not. Could you imagine having to take like a dozen men to court? Not that I know any of their names, but that alone gives me anxiety. Speaking of throw up, I got my first throw up on me tonight.

    One of my regulars came in tonight; he was telling me I smelled good and all that jazz and got his dance. Throughout the whole dance, he was looking woozy and lightheaded so I went out for a minute to get him some water—Who says strippers don't have a compassionate side? It was a good break for me anyhow. He was good with the water so I started dancing on him again, grinding good when he started sneezing out of nowhere and like hard and often. He was no longer erect, and this has never happened to me while dancing before. I wasn't sure what to do. In fact, all I remember thinking at this time was, Snot is better than jizz on my back. The dance wasn't even halfway done when all of a sudden vomit came like Mount Vesuvius on the top of my head…Yes, this is why I never get on my knees.

    I started crying because I didn't know what else to do. Yes, I was high, but I wasn't cracked out of my consciousness. The guy started yelling at me about being allergic to perfume? Told my manager he is going to sue me and the club for wearing perfume? I don't know what happened. I wear perfume every night, thinking he might be the one cracked out. This is the second time a guy has complained about perfume allergies. Are they really allergic, or are they just scared the scent of a stripper is going to go home with them? My manager told me not to worry about it and told me I needed to rinse my head under the sink. Yes, strippers are not allowed to leave their shift even if *vomited on; again, I suppose it's worse than jizz. Ugh, sick. No liquids in this house...Lord, help me.*

Love,

T

December 5, 2008

Dear Diary,

    Guess who showed up at my house before my shift tonight? Vic from my first club! He kept going off about how I owe him money and drugs and that I'd be lucky if I only ended up raped for the second time. He told me if I called the cops, he would go to my dad's house. He even had the address. I'm thinking he's all talk but still scary.

    Coincidentally, or not coincidentally, at the club tonight, this guy said his friend paid me a visit today? I was confused, or at least I played confused. The guy made a comment about my air mattress in my house. I was and still am beyond confused about it. The guy was creepy.

    So many other creepy guys to worry about though. Stripping is not fun; the movies lie. Burt Reynolds doesn't come in oiled up in cowboy boots and want to marry you and call you angel. No, you get guys who are illegal, guys who are in the mafia, who've been to prison, who are murderers. I had one guy tonight tell me he wanted to kill his wife, and ironically, I just so happened to look like his wife. He went on in a monologue about how he can't kill his wife, but he can kill a whore because nobody cares about whores? Had security walk me to my car all the way and stay. It's worth tipping twenty dollars for this.

    Talked to my mom, told her about still being sick. She thinks I haven't had enough fluids, probably true. I haven't been to the grocery store since Halloween. What's the point really? Had to lend some money to Superman; that was annoying, but at least he stopped calling.

Vic gives me the willies. I guess if I die, he'd be the one to blame. Maybe I was poisoned? That's what this feels like, food poisoning of some sort.

Love,
T

December 29, 2008

Dear Diary,

    Been back with my dad now for a couple weeks. He took me to the hospital December 19 after I called him when I couldn't even move to go to the bathroom. Lost about sixty pounds in the past year. Been shaking 'cause of withdrawals.

    I wasn't pregnant, thank goodness. That's all I was worried about when my dad was the one to take me to the hospital. He's going to pay me to start going back to school. It feels good to be protected from my manager and some of my shadier customers. My dad lives in a gated community. Nice to be on a break.

    My body is tired; my mind is fried. Going to start spending some time making more online videos. I do enjoy that. It'll be nice to save some money and do something other than drugs and sex. I feel like a little girl again, kind of refreshing.

Love,

T

April 15, 2009

Dear Diary,

I'm so happy I found this book again, rereading all my mess-ups in the past. Moved out of my dad's house and in with my mom and sister. Can't believe they are finally out here. It's nice not to have to focus on finding a guy to live with or doing the bills all on my own.

Went to a new strip club near us. My mom knows; my mom is kind of impressed with the money I make. This new strip club is fun. I pretend like I know nothing. I tell everyone it's my first time ever stripping, and I'm doing it for college and my (imaginary) daughter. Stripping is great for actors or compulsive liars, whatever way you look at it. Lots of Persians again in the valley. Lots of Persians and Mexicans and all the girls are black once again. I'm a rare gem here. Easy, easy money, no sex though, that shit is for the birds. I love that saying "for the birds."

Feels good to dance only when I need the money! No celebrities, kind of a dingy spot, but it'll do. Got to do a lot more auditions. The Eminem video I did came out a couple weeks ago. Got me a lot more jobs. Even started modeling for this fetish company.

Wore the corset into the club tonight. They love me there. This is the first club since the one I started at where I feel like a star. Got a gun in my car and pepper spray in my purse. A few girls tried to steal some shit. I took a piss in their purse after grabbing my phone out of it. They are so dumb. They do cheap drugs too, total amateurs.

Sharing a bed with my mom, too late to wake her up, so just going to sleep on the couch.

Love,

May 8, 2009

Dear Diary,

    Tonight was my twenty-first birthday, and I worked at my first club in NYC. I came here last night to see a show, a Broadway show with a very specific actor starring in it, "Rodd Thunder." Rodd was so brilliant. I didn't wait around to say hi. Heck, I haven't emailed him in almost two years. I just wanted to get away from LA, from family drama, from the mundane life that is mine. I'm happy, I suppose. Dancing in NYC is quite lame compared to LA. No sex, weak drugs, and all natural women. It's a different ball game. I went to the show with my drama teacher from high school. It was nice to see him again. Happy he could meet with me. He tried to get in my pants, but I'm so numb to any feeling, sexual or emotional, that I just couldn't. I told him I was tired and wanted to sleep, but he could have sex with me while I lay there. I think it weirded him out; I think I weirded him out. He called me this morning and asked to take me out to dinner for my birthday. I told him I was dancing. He thought I meant burlesque or like off Broadway. I told him the club, and he came by.

    I could see disappointment in his eyes. I was used to this feeling. I've disappointed a lot of people in my life. It almost was comforting to know I could count on myself to disappoint. Watching Rodd on stage last night and being myself on the strip club stage tonight made me realize that we're all just humans. We're all just trying to survive in this world. Rodd was a star in my eyes, but he was a nervous little thing inside of my world, just like I am in his world of entertainment. In the strip club, I'm a goddess; on a set, I'm merely background, a blur in the shot.

    Tried some drugs with a former club kid tonight, such a cliché NYC experience, but it was all fine. I'm doing a talk show tomorrow, hosted by this supermodel. See how that goes. New York is just not my style really. Lots of trash on the streets, lots of stares, and overall just a sense of boring. The only thing good here is live theater. I *remember having dreams of doing live theater as a girl. Not sure how I ended up here.*

Love,

T

June 20, 2009

Dear Diary,

I can't believe Brian is dead. This is so crazy. I loved Brian so much. All I could think about tonight while dancing is He'll never come in again. I'll never receive an email from him. I did all my sets to Alice Cooper music. I just started crying on stage.

This one dude yelled, "Alice Cooper sucks!" I wanted to kick him in the nuts so bad. I spit in his face, and the cops came, but I didn't get arrested because the guy said it was a misunderstanding. He was obviously in the country illegally.

Didn't get one dance tonight. I guess everyone could feel my depression. I want to do drugs so badly, but my health has sucked lately. I just want to feel numb, but I don't want to die.

Got to know my manager a little better tonight. He's actually kind of funny. His name is Mo, short for Mohammed. He even let me go home early. I like to make up stories about my life. I guess now I'm up to five kids of my own. The dancers tend to leave me alone now because they think I'm already fucked by having five kids at age twenty-one. Though I tell them I'm like thirty-five, hopefully make them feel less threatened. This club has closed down four times due to drugs, solicitation, a fistfight, a knife fight, and a shooting…I didn't know this until Mo told me, so trying to just play nice.

Still in shock over Brian's death. It's weird. I can't fathom this. Like he's the one person I have to email, the one friend in my life. Why would he do this? Why would anyone do this?

Love,

June 29, 2009

Dear Diary,

Tonight, one of the girls played Michael Jackson music in honor of his memory. Took me back to being a little girl. I was literally on stage, completely naked, dancing to one of his songs, and all I could think about was driving up with my father when I was twelve to see Michael Jackson's house up north. My dad drove me three hours there and back just to look at Michael Jackson's gate and wait outside in hopes of seeing him. We never did. But my dad just waited with me until I said I was done. I got another flash while I was just sitting watching another girl dance to a track. The flash of my dad waiting outside the Santa Maria courthouse during Michael Jackson's trials. My dad was never a patient man. He always had a temper most of the time I can recall growing up, but he would stay with me and drive me up there until I said I was tired. He didn't even like Michael Jackson. My dad always thought he was weird. He supported me though and my love for him. My dad's a good guy. I just wish we understood each other better.

I had to get high. I couldn't go through this somber time any other way. Each dance was making me feel more and more depressed. The thought of losing Brian and then Michael Jackson, for some reason, it took me to this dark place of losing my father and my mother and my brother and my sister. I kept thinking what would happen if they were no longer in my life because they were no longer on this earth. Even as I'm penning this, I can't help but sob. I need to reach out. I need to keep the connection open between my family.

Life is not about money, not about sex or drugs or dancing. Life is about living to please God, living to make others happy. I wasn't making others happy. I don't find joy in pretending to care about people's lives just for their money; that's not happiness.

Family is happiness. Love is happiness. Why can't I find love? I'm going to have to give myself this love for now, just for now...but hopefully not forever.

Love,

T

July 4, 2009

Dear Diary,

When you lose someone you love so unexpectedly, it's devastating. I can't eat or sleep. I've been having sex with anyone for free. It's hard to breathe. Every day, it's a challenge to breathe. I just want my only friend back. I even reached out to Michael again today, still no response. Nobody loves me, nobody. My mom and sister are giving me headaches. I feel like all I have is the club. At the club, I am anybody I want to be and everybody the world wants me to be. Tonight, I was half Filipino, and within an hour, I was half black with a Muslim background.

Need a change, need to get away. Went to church this morning for guidance and direction and purpose. We had another underage girl start today. This is the second one at this club—seems to be a common theme in LA clubs. I was devastated. Would she turn out like me? Hard and washed up at twenty-one years old? I don't trust any man—or any person. Everyone is out to get me, everyone. I don't like food. I only want to inject myself and have unprotected sex. I go to daily Mass. I am fucked up in my head.

Brian would always say I was fucked; he was right. How did this happen? How did I get here? Thank goodness for the Internet. Posting videos on there is the only glimpse I have of the real Trish. The Trish that loves herself and loves to entertain. Thinking I might have developed multiple personality disorder through all this. My mom is worried about me even though she doesn't say it.

Tonight, the air broke in the club and I just about died. I only made fifty dollars, and that's with extra. I'm so done. I'm so exhausted. I just want to go to sleep...forever.

Love,

July 29, 2009

Dear Diary,

God is good. I may be taking a break from this journal to do a new journal, a prayer journal. God has blessed me with a clean bill of health, for once, and two jobs on television. I am feeling alive. I took my mom and sister out to dinner. It just feels good to connect with myself again. I made a few hundred dollars from my videos this month; it's so crazy to be getting paid to entertain strangers. It's kind of what I have always wanted.

Someone at the club recognized me from my tanning addiction show tonight. Felt good and bad at the same time. They asked me why I was working here. I answered with the truth, "I don't know." Why am I working here? This is not what God put me on this earth to do, is it? If one good thing has come of me being a stripper, it is sharing my stories with my younger sister. She never wants to be a stripper; she told me tonight via text. She said she is scared for me and is going to be going to college next semester so she won't ever have to. I was proud of her. I think we always thought stripping was a good idea based off what we'd seen in Lifetime movies and such, but real life is so depressing in the sex industry. I have cystic acne, meth scars, tattered clothes, and a purse full of piss every night.

A nice older gentleman at the club tonight offered to take me away from all this. He said he'd pay for my company but he was also looking for a wife. I just don't think I could do that for money, not anymore. I realized life is about finding my own happiness. I need to make myself happy, and God will provide the rest as needed. I need more faith. I love the men who come into our clubs because no one else will. All the souls in strip clubs need the most prayers because they are lacking something, somewhere, even if it's buried deep. Redemption shall come, and I will love every soul I encounter. I have forgiven all the rapists, the pedophiles, the stalkers, and all the others who have made my life hell. I only pray they find God and repent before it's too late.

Love,

T

August 2, 2009

Dear Diary,

    Tonight was an interesting night. I got asked out by Mo's friend Amir, and I said yes? Kind of weird, but I like him. He always gives me a lot of money, but that's not why I like him. He has a thick accent and is very tall and always respectful. He's not my type at all, but I'm excited to go out with him.

    Spent hours just talking in the VIP room that he paid for; the girls are super jealous. All my makeup was missing from my broken-lock locker, and someone took a piss in my bag. What's with strippers acting like fucking trashy cats? It's weird. It's like they're not human beings.

    Amir is sweet, though I could never date him long term. He's Muslim; I'm Catholic. That sounds like the beginning of a joke: a Muslim and a Catholic walk into a strip club...haha. Sadly, this is my life.

    Hopefully no one finds out we're dating outside the club. Even though it's totally ghetto, I kind of like this club. It feels like home in a weird way. Plus, it's the easiest money I've ever made. It's close to my house, and even when I look my worst, I'm still the hottest one in this place. Pretty uneventful night. Think Kid Rock came in...could be mistaken, but it looked like him. Heard he loves the black chicks, so it would make sense.

    Been clean for a few weeks now, feeling proud of myself. Cleaning up my act, working on Internet videos during the day, feels like a schedule, sort of.

    See how tomorrow goes.

Love,

August 14, 2009

Dear Diary,

    Today, I worked the day shift, first time in a long time doing that. It wasn't so bad. Made a couple hundred dollars and gave half to my mom for her birthday. Amir took us all out to eat. He is very kind and sweet. My mom likes him. I don't get butterflies for him. To be honest, I really am just trying to keep him as my customer and no one else's. Nonetheless, I care a lot about him as a human being and am not trying to lead him on. He even came in for my entire shift today. Got a little in trouble by my manager because I spent the whole time talking to him, but I was able to snatch up some dances to keep the club happy. Amir keeps me company. He bought me new shoes from next door and had chicken fingers delivered for me. He is a great guy.

    This poor, sweet sixteen-year-old can't seem to make a buck. I caught her stealing an iPod and some jewelry, probably fake, from some of the girls' bags that they leave in there. I carry around a full purse with me. I don't even care. I don't trust anyone. I didn't say anything, but I offered her some of my tips and some advice. I told her to stay away from drugs because if she was desperate for money now, stealing from strippers, drugs would ruin her in a whole other way. She called me old and washed up, which was crazy, and threatened to steal my car. It makes me sad that this girl is in there. I pray for her. I really do. She is too beautiful to be in this industry. I saw her having sex with a man who was probably sixty and walked with a limp. I know he doesn't have much money, and he also smells like green beans. My heart literally breaks in half.

    Other than that, pretty uneventful. Thank God for my family and even for Amir; he's keeping me company and employed.

Love,

T

August 22, 2009

Dear Diary,

This club is dangerous. It doesn't feel right anymore—not that it ever did, but I feel terrified going in. My paranoia is at an all-time high for some reason. I keep having visions of me getting killed. I want these thoughts out of my head. I don't want them to manifest, but they are so graphic and so visual. I can't sleep at night. I shake when I'm awake. Maybe it's coming off drugs, but it feels more than that. It feels real.

I asked Amir if he thought I was ever going to get out of this club, out of stripping. He said he knew I was. He bought me this beautiful pearl necklace, and I knew it was real because it smelled like pearls. The smell of real pearls is something I can't describe, but I remember smelling my mother's pearls my dad had given her and just thought they smelled luxurious. Between him telling me I was meant for better things and giving me such an extravagant gift, I thought about all these angels in disguise, Amir, Pearl, and I still believe the world is mostly full of good people even in the seedy world of strip clubs and prostitution. Amir is a no-bullshit kind of guy. He doesn't promise me marriage; he doesn't promise me the world. I don't love him, but I love what he does for me.

Something in my life is missing. Something's got to give, but what? What am I doing wrong? The constant battle of my life is right versus wrong. I know what I'm doing is not good, but I can't quit. There's a mental illness brewing, and I wasn't born with it. How fitting that Taxi Driver is on now. It's very disturbing that I now can understand Travis Bickle's thought process. Need sleep.

Love,

T

September 10, 2009

Dear Diary,

    Michael got arrested this past week. I reached out to him, and he wanted to hang out again. Oh my goodness, I am so happy! I took the whole weekend off work and went back tonight for the first time. He kept texting me through the whole night.

    I was in the middle of a lap dance with this super creep, Al, who comes in all the time just to jerk off in front of me, and I even texted in the middle of that. Michael just makes me smile. I told him I quit dancing but that I work on my Internet videos at night and have deadlines, or something along those lines. I just want to marry and have babies with him. I make enough off my videos for a part-time job. I guess in theory I could quit dancing. I want to so badly. Michael suspects me of being on drugs though. He judges me for doing them, even though he chain-smokes weed. If I got pregnant, I would quit it all, and he would have to too. My head is just spinning with so much excitement.

    Told my manager Tia all about getting back together with him. She told me I was being stupid because I have a dozen guys touching me every night for money. She doesn't get it. She's a little fat Guatemalan woman who tells all the Mexicans I'm a prostitute in Spanish. I'm so much more than a hooker, a stripper, a druggie, a junkie, like I'm meant to do great things.

    Had a man come in tonight and tell me he was a prophet. He told me I was going to burn in hell if I didn't quit what I was doing. I think I'm going to quit for good. Like, this is too much to deal with. Aside from that, two girls got arrested tonight, not sure why. The cops took us all in the back room to search our lockers. I bolted out of there.

Between the prophet and Michael coming back into my life, I think I'm going to take a leap of faith and just quit and pray that either marriage comes into play or my Internet videos will take off.

Love,

T

September 17, 2009

Dear Diary,

    Had this older lady come in tonight asking for me. It threw me off at first. She knew me by my music taste. She said she'd been watching me for a while and wanted a dance. It was unconventional, and it was a first for me. I had never given a dance to a woman by herself. She wasn't part of a couple or a party. It was just her. She offered me a couple thousand to go home with her. I looked at her. I stared at her. She was beautiful, but you knew she was a knockout in her prime. Her facial structure was perfection, her smell was intoxicating, and she had designer everything from head to toe. I was confused. I was flattered, but I was sad. What was this woman's story?

    I often wonder that about anybody who comes into the club but her especially. I declined her offer, but I can't stop thinking about her. When I was dancing, she was quivering as if she was nervous, and I'm not sure why. She squirmed a lot and kept clutching her thighs tightly together. She tipped me amazing and gave me a kiss on the lips. Another first tonight. I was questioning my sexuality. Maybe guys mistreated me because I'm not supposed to end up with a male. My church tells me being gay is wrong, so how am I feeling this? I pray not to explore this but rather get over it. Is this something I can get over?

    She told me my boyfriend was a lucky man. I don't know how she sensed I had a boyfriend or if she was just assuming, but I'm the lucky one to be with him. Right? I don't know. I hope it lasts, but I feel like I'm searching for something that may never be found. I feel like this woman was the same way. It's almost as if she was me in thirty years. It tripped me out. Her kiss was one of the most amazing things I've felt in a long while.

Love,

T

September 20, 2009

Dear Diary,

    Keeping a positive mind when working at a strip club is a very challenging thing. I love my boyfriend so much. I really wish I could make my full-time living doing something else, but what? My mom brought me takeout tonight. She said it was her first time in a strip club, and she just wanted to see where I was, what kind of atmosphere I was in. I think she was hurt, but more than that, I think she was sad for me. I think she was more disappointed in herself than with me. She held me so long when she dropped off the food, and she started crying, which of course led me to crying. I told her it was going to be OK. I was the one always reassuring her. She may not have been the best example going from husband to husband, baby daddy to baby daddy, but ultimately, this was my choice.

    My mom also brought in this diary. She told me it was on the floor after she washed our sheets. It must've been under my pillow this morning. She said she didn't read it, and I said she could. She told me she didn't want to know. She asked me to share it with the underage girl we had working in the club. Maybe she could learn something. I never told my mom specifics of what has happened over the years, but a mother just has intuition about these kinds of things.

    I thought about sharing some stories, heck, I even think about just giving her this book, but I don't think she'll listen. Who would listen? I feel like I'm still such a mess, but I feel like if I could go back and share my stories with thirteen-year-old or sixteen-year-old me, I would be in a very different place. Maybe it's too late for me, but maybe it's not too late for another young Trish somewhere in the Midwest. Maybe I'll share these in a blog or something, nothing too graphic, just enough so people can sense the unhappiness. That strippers aren't all going to get the happily ever after they get in movies, even if they do have a heart of gold. Maybe one day, I'll be in a place where I can *share with someone who'll listen. But not this girl, or maybe? I don't know. Think about it. Tired as per usual.*

Love,

T

September 30, 2009

Dear Diary,

The end is near. Not for my life—at least I pray not—but for getting out of this industry. I cannot explain what I'm feeling. I wish I could. I wish I could just purge all this emotion out right now. I don't know where I'm going or what I'm doing, but I know the end is near for me. The time for me to do great things is coming. Nothing is fun about dancing anymore. Nothing excites me. Nothing turns me on. I'm numb. Michael cheated yet again, and here I am, thinking about him, hoping he'll still want to be with me. Such bullshit. Yet, how can I ask for respect when I don't even respect myself?

I've never respected myself until this moment. In this very moment, I'm getting that urgency I felt as a girl in my small town of wanting to get out to show the world how amazing I am. I am amazing. I am so amazing, and I am wasting this life. The day of reckoning is coming. The day where I can feel freed. Up until now, my entire adult life has been a prison, and I've been the only one who could release me.

I didn't do any dances tonight. Mo threatened to fire me if I didn't at least attempt to get dances, but I didn't care. I observed the customers. I observed the girls. I observed Mo. How did we all get here? What happened in our lives that we have come to this hellhole on earth? Some guys looked bored; some looked eager. Some girls looked beautiful, while others looked beat up. I saw the pimps come in. I saw the regulars. The staff was like robots to me. The whole world seemed like another world tonight. Nothing seemed real. Tonight was the first night I didn't feel like I belonged in there, and I don't. I'm not sure how to break out of this or why. What's going to click for me finally? When am I finally going to say, 'Enough'? I pray to God right now that these answers will come. I may not be the smartest girl, but I know I'm better than this.

Love,

T

October 1, 2009

Dear Diary,

Tonight, I had a therapy session at the club. A sweet older gentleman, a retired psychologist, came in. The first thing he said to me was that I was too pretty to be in a club like this. To which I told him, he was too kind to be in a club like this. We got to talking, and he was so intelligent. He picked up on so many things about me without me having to tell him much of anything. He was quite the charmer; I can't lie. I told him I thought I was going crazy from dancing. Never been this honest with a customer, but I knew it was time to start being honest in life in general, so why not start now? It has to be the first step in getting out of this dump.

He told me it's not uncommon for nurture over nature to make someone's mental state a little off. He knew quite a few people who came from the best upbringing but due to circumstances throughout life, they lost a few screws. He told me what's important is that I'm acknowledging the change and that I can still fix it, still redeem who I am.

I actually told him my real name, and he thought it was lovely. He told me I had a face for television and that if he were younger, he'd marry me. It's a funny thing, this would've always excited me in the past, but I realized I don't want to be married, not right now. I'm not happy with myself. How would I make anyone else happy? I just smiled and giggled.

He got a dance from me, and he got hard from it. I don't know what it is, but erections just ruin any sincere moments that might've happened. I guess when it comes down to it, we're all just sexual beings and that's just the way we were made. Well, except for me. Pretty sure I'm not gay or straight, just asexual.

We also had a girl tonight wear a burlap bag on stage. She really liked it, and then she walked around biting people. I don't know why *this stuck with me. I just thought it was random and funny. She was happy though. She was laughing her ass off every time I spotted her.*

Love,
T

October 11, 2009

Dear Diary,

    I am shaking like a leaf. I can't stop crying, and I just had to burst out to my mom and sister. This little sixteen-year-old girl who was working at our club wasn't sixteen; she was in fact fourteen, and she was killed tonight. Right outside our club, not more than a half a block down the street on Sepulveda. She was shot seven times, and I'm hysterical. Apparently, it's a guy who comes into our club all the time. We heard the shots, and I wanted to bolt, but I realized we didn't even have a back entrance. The shooter came into our club, and thank goodness the manager locked the door to the dressing room. He was yelling and demanding to see a girl named Amanda. I don't know if that was a girl's real name or what but we had no stripper named Amanda at our club. Apparently, the fourteen-year-old was Amanda, but he was out of his mind and didn't realize he had already killed her. Security had called the cops, and they were in there. I think all of us, even the girls on crack, were terrified. We all huddled together in one sweaty, meth-filled group. I got next to this girl, Fame, whom I had always looked at as the most beautiful girl in our club, one of the highest-paid girls, and when I was close to her, I smelled the booze on her breath and the odor from her vagina and saw her teeth were literally decaying so thin, her tongue moving caused enamel to shed.

    Mo told all of us to go home and if we wanted to work, to go to the club that they owned next to the airport. He walked me to my car as he did all the girls and told me not to be swayed by what had happened there that night. He was so calm and nonchalant about it. If I ever needed a sign, this was it. No more. God was speaking to me. He told me that I was putting my life in danger, and if I loved him, I would stop what I was doing and let him provide what I needed. This world is too beautiful to be wasted. I need nothing else in this very moment but my health, my family, and God. I'm done.

Love,

T

January 23, 2012

Dear Diary,

 Today, I broke down; I told my dad about my past. I ran out of gas and was too embarrassed to just ask for cash, so I had a meltdown. When my dad cut me off at eighteen—I never asked for a single penny...but I was stuck.

 I cried. I sobbed. I let myself feel hurt and pain for once in my life. When I drove back to his house to write a check to him for cash, his wife (who's the reason I was kicked out in the first place) was just standing there with that look of attack that's always in her eyes whenever I'm around.

 Went into my dad's office and put the check down saying I needed cash. I was so humiliated. He ripped up the check and just handed me forty dollars; I lost it. He has never handed me money since the day I quit college. I started hyperventilating. It felt like a panic attack, even though I had never experienced one before. I couldn't catch my breath. I ran to my car and drove off. My dad got in his and followed. I pulled into the gas station, and my dad filled up my tank with his credit card and asked if we could talk at the McDonald's next door.

 We talked for two hours over two coffees. I had yelled out in my disarray that I couldn't afford my medications, that all the health problems I suffered from were the direct result of poor choices as a stripper years ago. My dad was hurt but remained strong. He offered to help with my medical expenses and told me to offer up my struggles and pain on this earth to God, that he'd do everything he could to help me.

 My father has always been there for me, and I disappointed him yet again. Seeing pain in your parent's eye is the worst heartache. I love you, Dad.

Love,

T

Printed in Great Britain
by Amazon.co.uk, Ltd.,
Marston Gate.